Jacaranda Festival

Grafton's Purple Trees

Spring is here.

Look at the trees.
The trees in our town
are special.
They are very, very old.

5

We have a festival

in our town,

to celebrate the trees.

At the festival,

there are flowers everywhere.

Flowers are here

and here

and here.

This is the clock in our town.

At the festival,

we put a **crown**

on the clock.

LIBRARY
MOTELS C/VAN PK.

At the festival,
we wear purple clothes.

At the festival,

we eat purple **ice-cream**.

Glossary

crown

ice-cream